# SIMPLE WORDS FOR TROUBLED TIMES

MESSAGES OF HOPE AND COMFORT

RONEN GROVES

PHILLIPA NEFRI CLARK WRITING AS RONEN GROVES

Copyright © 2020 by Phillipa Nefri Clark writing as Ronen Groves

All rights reserved. By payment of the required fees, you have been granted the non-exclusive, non-transferable right to access and read the text of this e-book on-screen. No part of this text may be reproduced, transmitted, downloaded, decompiled, reverse engineered, or stored in or introduced into any information storage and retrieval system, in any form or by any means, whether electronic or mechanical, now known or hereinafter invented, without the express written permission of the publisher and the author.

Cover by Book Cover Zone

Editing by Nas Dean

*This work does not offer professional or medical advice. The author makes no claims for outcomes from following suggestions therein and recommends all readers use their own judgement on what may work for them.*

## SIMPLE WORDS FOR TROUBLED TIMES

**The world we know has turned upside-down.**

Everything we've taken for granted changed before there was time to take stock. We have had to adjust. To adapt. To survive.

For some this brings a sense of helplessness. Others feel grief and anger. All of us are affected.

*Simple Words for Troubled Times* is written from the heart to help you find comfort and relief from the challenges of modern times.

Each short chapter addresses a different means to rebuild hope, rediscover self-belief, reinforce your personal power, and redirect fears into courage.

There is no greater power than a simple word of hope.

## CONTENTS

| | |
|---|---|
| 1. Changing the Lens | 1 |
| 2. Reconnections | 4 |
| 3. Your Power | 6 |
| 4. The Did-do List | 9 |
| 5. You Matter | 12 |
| 6. Wallowing | 15 |
| 7. Perfect Moments | 19 |
| 8. The Worth of Worry | 21 |
| 9. Dreams to Do | 25 |
| 10. It is Around You, Not Inside You | 28 |
| 11. Doing Well When Things Get Tight | 30 |
| 12. Silver Linings | 35 |
| 13. Accept Regrets | 39 |
| 14. A Secret Oasis | 43 |
| 15. Be Fearless | 46 |
| 16. Gratitude, Joy and Resilience | 49 |
| Afterword | 53 |
| About the Author | 55 |
| By Phillipa Nefri Clark | 57 |

## 1

## CHANGING THE LENS

*We can perceive anything as negative or positive.
Choose your lens.*

What do you see when you look outside? Houses, trees, the side of a building, a city, open land, the ocean?

Now consider the inside of your home. There are rooms, furniture, books, appliances, carpet. Perhaps washing to fold or vacuuming to do.

When we see the same things all the time they fade into the background unless we have reason to inspect more closely.

Look in a mirror at the reflection you've seen your whole life. Are there lines around your mouth? Do you wish they weren't there or do you appreciate them because they formed from a lifetime of laughter and expression?

How we view something is critical to its impact on us. It is easy to see an object, a situation, or ourselves at face value. The lens we look through colors our response. Depending upon the lens, this might vary from neutral to negative, or regret to rejoicing. Here's an example.

*This house is old. It needs painting and some repairs. The floor creaks in the hallway. Overgrown trees block the view to the street.*

### Let's try changing the lens

*This house has a sense of history because this is where you raised a family. It could use some TLC but was built to last. Hearing that familiar creak late at night lets you know the last of the family are safely home. Those beautiful old trees gives privacy.*

Which lens is accurate? Both are, but the second one gives some perspective and depth to the same situation.

Think about how you view something. Anything. An annoying task or your dream vocation. Write down in a few words what it means to you. Does it weigh you down, interfere with other more important things? Are you pursuing your dream and if not, why not. Make a short list using as many descriptive words as you want.

Time to rewrite the list. First, change the lens. Put a positive in front of each statement. Instead of 'the washing needs folding again and I'm the only one who does it', try 'I can do this as I plan dinner or watch TV'. Or 'Learning guitar is so hard. I'm no good at it', try 'I love how practicing makes me feel'.

Do you see the difference? A subtle change of approach turns negative to positive. Such a simple technique and applicable to almost every aspect of our lives. Look around and find something in your room that you treat as a negative.

*The bookcase is a mess.* (Negative)

### Turn it around

*I can't wait to revisit my favorite authors as I put them back in order.* (Positive)

Even if you say the words aloud and don't believe them at the time, your mind will recognize the optimism. Our brains are clever things and reward us with good feelings if we smile or speak with an upbeat tone. Singing and dancing have similar effects.

Rephrase statements. Use "I love", "I will", "I am worthy" instead of less flattering words.

You deserve to see yourself and your life through a positive lens. You are worth it and those who love you will agree.

*Rephrase negative thoughts and statements Actively search for ways to see the good in life
Be proud of who you are and what you do*

## 2

## RECONNECTIONS

*We are never apart if we can connect*

Our world is more than a planet we live upon. It is the society around us, the community where we reside, friends and our family, workmates and acquaintances we see in passing.

Beyond this is a greater network across the globe, whether people we've met in real life living far away, social media friends, or pen pals from the past.

Who are you connected to?

Think of every person you know. If you like, write down any names which come to mind. Begin with your immediate family and extend it out to distant relatives.

Then your closest friends and their friends and family. Once you add people you've worked with, gone to school with, had business dealings with, and any other number of situations, the list is long.

Not everyone has close friends and family. But we all have connections to other humans.

What an incredible network. It makes the world feel smaller when we think of knowing so many of its inhabitants.

*Even social media has its place*

Anytime you feel alone or lonely, lost or sad, remember these amazing connections. Reach out to them. Some you may have little in common with but we all have current world events as a shared experience. We know it is keeping us physically apart from others, but on the flipside it presents the perfect opportunity to say hello, how are you?

Is there someone you'd love to talk to? Even if just to laugh about old times and compare notes about home schooling or missing your daily routine. Don't put it off. Make the phone call, set up a video chat, send a message or a letter.

If there's a fence to mend, then do it. Odds are if you miss someone, they miss you too. And if it is family, then don't waste a minute. In uncertain times, *re*connecting is key.

We're not going to track down every person we know. But if each of us reconnects with a few people who've slipped out of our focus, and then they do the same, and each of those people does…you get the drift.

Before you know it, you'll feel the warmth and good wishes from a world full of people who care about you. We are never apart if we can connect.

*Remember the people you know*
*Be fearless in reaching out with friendship and love*
*Reconnect to keep your network strong*

# 3

## YOUR POWER

*Believe it when nobody else does*

You have incredible power.

It lives deep within you.

Beneath the layers of life laid down each passing season is an undeniable truth. *You* are a powerful being.

As babies, our power is in our helplessness. Our tears and cries and needs are our superpower over those who care for us, for without that attention and love and nurturing we would die. But we are fed and changed and cuddled and carried because the natural power of a human baby controls those much bigger and stronger adults around us.

Over the years, through childhood and adolescence, this primal power became unacceptable to society. We are no longer cute and helpless. We are expected to grow up, manage our fears, deal with our problems quietly and above all, bury our power.

So we do. We force down our feelings so not to upset or offend, or perhaps we go the other way and use our words as weapons to control others by inflicting emotional pain. Some even use weapons as weapons. We seek acceptance and approval and want to get more things. All the time. More.

*Is all lost? How do we rediscover it?*

When we lose touch with our natural power, we are like a boat in a storm with a broken mast. Still built for the job but floating where the tides and winds dictate. At any moment we might sink. We grab at anything to keep us afloat. To make us feel strong. Think of what you have gathered around yourself to feel strong. Is it money? Prestige? Misuse of food or alcohol or drugs? Are you trapped in a job or relationship you hate because you feel…powerless?

Consider our boat in the storm. Like every boat, it has a small, unremarkable part. A rudder. Like our own natural power, in the right hands a rudder will steer even a damaged boat to safety. No broken mast will stop us if we remember we have an internal rudder, a perfect power ready to keep our path strong and true.

Power is not loud nor violent. It is neither showy nor excessive. It doesn't build you up by pulling down another person. We are trained to believe power is for the wealthy, for superstars or sporting heroes. For politicians and governments and CEO's of giant companies.

How is one person, one ordinary person, powerful?

*Your power is in your authenticity*

Find a place of calm to dig deep into your memories. Lay on the floor or close your eyes in the shower, it doesn't matter where or how, but look inside yourself. Bypass the self-doubt and push aside the voices of those who tell us we are less than powerful.

Ask your mind where your power lives.

A baby *has no choice* but to be powerful.

The power of an adult is not in tears or cries or helplessness. It is more subtle.

It is discovering who you are at the core. The authentic you.

Are there words that ring true when you whisper them to yourself? Words such as kind? Determined? Loving? Caring? Brave? Funny? Seek the positive words to describe yourself and listen to your heart when you say them. You'll know when you find the right ones.

Those words are your power. Practice saying them to yourself and use them to build your self-confidence and belief. Use them as a rudder when external forces buffet you like a storm. They are a building block and will never, ever fail you.

*You* have incredible power.

*Ask yourself where your perfect power lies*
*Call on it to protect yourself against bad influences*
*Practice being powerful*

# 4

## THE DID-DO LIST

*A list that gives real joy*

We all know about **to-do** lists.

Scribbled reminders on post-it notes, or the back of envelopes, a whiteboard near the fridge or a notepad near the computer. Or even on our phones. Pay the bills, do the shopping, put out the washing, bring in the washing, clean the pantry, bath the dog or the kids or both, mop the floors, mow the grass, service the car, reply to emails, organize the cupboard…it goes on and on.

Even if we cross off everything on each list, the satisfaction is short lived as we start the next long line of things needing our attention. The reality is that for most of us, to-do lists are little more than a reminder of work ahead and are neither fun nor interesting. And if we look back on them, it is the same old thing over and over.

What if we created a **did-do** list.

Every time you complete something important, difficult,

challenging, wonderful, or put off for ages, write it on a square of paper and drop it into a jar or unused vase or any type of transparent container. You could use different colored paper for different types of tasks.

Choose a timeframe to revisit these. It is in your hands whether you want to do it weekly, monthly, yearly. Even on a special occasion such as New Year's Eve or the anniversary of moving to a new house. Or at those moments of feeling you don't achieve much. These little squares will remind you just how much you have accomplished. How well you've done.

Would any of these be on your did-do list?

*Learned to meditate*
*Stopped smoking*
*Read a book*
*Helped a friend*
*Lost or gained weight as planned*
*Knitted a jumper*
*Planted seedlings*
*Created a recipe*
*Finished a jigsaw*
*Painted the house*

Now, imagine yourself reading all your did-do's in one sitting. Some achievements might bring a smile and others will remind you how hard you worked or studied to make it happen. Allow yourself to feel proud. Celebrate.

Even little things such as tending to overdue sewing, weeding the garden, cleaning the car, washing the dog all add up to lots of positives.

When you write down what you've done *after* it is finished, it reinforces your satisfaction or relief of completion. And when you read about it later, so much the better.

Much more fun and rewarding than crossing off an endless, repetitive list.

> *Be proud of what you've accomplished*
> *Encourage the family to play along*
> *Appreciate your achievements*

## 5

## YOU MATTER

*Do you put others first, or yourself last?*
*There's a difference.*

So often we put ourselves last. Not always on purpose, but the love we have for those around us makes it natural to put their needs before ours. Such a beautiful thing to be able to do. We see them thriving, going forward in their lives, achieving goals, and having time to relax. Whether you are a parent, a carer, or a friend, you want those you love to do well.

Sometimes, this carries over into other areas of our life. Work, social groups, hobbies, and other areas we interact and might continue putting other people first.

In principal, selflessness is a wonderful gift. If it fulfils us and brings happiness then it is good for us as well as those, we gift it too.

But what if it goes too far? If instead of putting others first, our mindset changes to putting ourselves last. It becomes a habit. A certain comfort comes from being the one who is last.

Last to sit down at the table. Last to go to bed because there are chores to finish. The one who misses out on a treat because you insist everyone else has extra.

*Are there times you feel invisible?*

Are you putting others first, or yourself last? There is a difference.

When we put everyone else ahead of ourselves, all the time, no matter why or how much we love them, it is at the risk of losing part of ourselves. Others become accustomed to the role we've chosen and may take us for granted. Without meaning to, others may take advantage of our kind hearts.

Are you a giver? Do you ensure those around you are comfortable and happy before attending your own needs, even important ones? Has it become a duty?

*You matter*

It is easy to back ourselves into a corner over time. Make a niche for ourselves and do it so well that nobody notices those times you do need to come first. Because we all deserve equal care and love and attention. You are every bit as precious to your family and friends as they are to you. Let them do the spoiling sometimes. Give them another gift. One of stepping up.

How to bring some balance depends on how willing you are to change. Yes, you. Not them. We teach people how we wish to be treated. If we are mean and cold then we're teaching people to avoid getting close to us. And if we are giving and selfless and insist on another person's needs being more important than ours, then they will learn to expect this. One step at a time, practice saying no, or asking for what you need. They may be surprised and sometimes, change is confronting. If they are upset or don't understand, a smile and few words about your wish to practice some self-care goes a long way.

*They matter as well.*

It is fine to reassure others you still love them and will always be there. Be calm and persistent and make changes slowly. Ask for help after dinner instead of automatically washing up alone. Or take up the hobby you've always wanted and let your loved ones know how much it means to you. Show them you are happy in being a little bit selfish.

If you find you are putting yourself last to keep peace in a difficult situation, please reach out to a trusted friend or organization for outside help. You deserve this.

People who love us will support and encourage our dreams. When we've conditioned them to not expect us to have dreams, or need a hand, then we have a bit of work to do. Having 'me time' is good for the soul and the mind. How much do you have?

*Recognize when you are taking too much on*
*Teach loved ones a different way to see you*
*Embrace yourself as a person. Remember you matter.*

# 6

## WALLOWING

*It is okay to not be okay as long as you don't give up*

Sometimes it all feels too hard.

Our best attempts to protect ourselves from distressing situations fails. We devour every bit of bad news until our eyes won't leave the TV or computer and our heart races but we keep watching. Listening. Speculating.

It gets to us. Worry. Stress. Fear. Helplessness. Is it even worth getting out of bed, dressing, taking care of ourselves? Or we might react by keeping everything in our sphere of influence normal, but falling apart inside. Either way we know we aren't handling things and might feel angry with ourselves, or guilty for not being stronger.

You probably ask your friends and family how they are out of concern for their wellbeing and state of mind.

But how do *you* answer those questions?

Do you tell your loved ones you are fine? Or fall into a heap the minute a sympathetic ear is around. For most of us, it is somewhere in between. Even when we feel so bad that focusing on the positives is impossible, we hold it together the best we can.

*Your best is always good enough*

Always.

Even if you can't see tomorrow, you know in your heart it will come. The sun will set and rise again. The passage of time will gradually heal us because nothing stays the same. It is finding a way to hold onto this truth, which is hard, when all we want is to bury our heads beneath a blanket.

Do you need to be strong all the time? If we have children or others we care for it is important to protect them from an overload of often inappropriate information. We don't like them seeing us upset. But it is also important to teach them about emotions and how it is normal to experience a myriad of confusing feeling when under duress. A fine balance at the best of times.

What is going on when we hit that wall and everything feels too hard?

Perhaps we call it self-pity. Being sorry for yourself. Self-absorbed. What about wallowing? This implies a short indulgent break from our normal, responsible, and logical self. We jump in, wiggle around in a make-believe mud bath for a bit and let the sorrows wash over us. Sounds kind of inviting.

Instead of holding your chin up and nodding while gritting your teeth every time someone says we should be grateful for what we have, when you already know that but have had enough of hearing it, go to your mud bath. Or a clear mountain stream, or hot tub. Wherever your mental 'wallow' spot exists, give yourself permission to visit.

*Let yourself spend a day in bed or in your pajamas.*

*Indulge in chocolate or your preferred comfort food.*

*Read all day with your feet up.*

*Have a good cry.*

*Write down all the things you are upset about and then throw it away.*

*Phone a friend. One who will sympathize and let you talk. Then return the favor.*

Our brains are clever. They protect us from harm in all kind of ways, such as urging us to move out of physical danger by our flight response. It tinkers around in the background, in our subconscious and dreams. When there is unusual duress, our brain may lessen its attention to complicated tasks or difficult plans. This makes us feel our focus isn't sharp but is perfectly normal.

If we listen to our body when it is physically tired, we rest. Ignoring it to push on and on results in exhaustion and collapse. The same applies to our emotional and mental health. When all you want is to hide from the world, it is your mind asking for a break. If you take no notice and allow the stress to build to breaking point, you might fall much further than having a day or so to rest and repair.

Listen to yourself. Take note of what you need and rather than push yourself for the sake of appearances or not upsetting someone else, give yourself some time to wallow. Visit that metaphorical mud bath or pool beneath a waterfall.

Use your time to reconnect with little things that matter. Listen to music you've forgotten about. Read a childhood book you cherish. Look through a photo album which you know makes you smile. Feel your way back to a more comfortable state. Appreciate your body for insisting you need a little break. Be okay with not always being okay.

*Your best is always good enough*
*Find a mental place to comfort yourself in*
*Never give up on yourself. You rock.*

7
---

# PERFECT MOMENTS

*They are your future memories.*

What is your favorite memory? Your wedding? A newborn in arms? A sunset?

Cast your mind back to that moment in time and draw on all your senses to relive it.

Where are you? Indoors or out? Is it daytime or night? Who is with you, or are you on your own?

Focus on the aromas. Whether food, or fresh rain, the ocean, or a flower, our ability to remember smell—and remember moments based on smell—is remarkable.

Are you warm, or wrapped up against the cold? Can you still taste what you ate and drank?

Ask yourself why this moment, of all moments in your life, is so memorable.

You lived it to the full. For you to recall even minor details, your *mind was present* in the moment of what is now your treasured memory.

Think about it. The strongest happy memories are ones we

truly embrace. We have the power to make heart-warming future memories every day, by noticing happiness, or good news, or the taste of a delightful recipe. Be aware of moments you want to relive and practice savoring them as you experience them.

*Be in the moment. Embrace it.*

Smell the aromas.

What do your fingertips tell you?

If there is music playing, pay it attention. When you hear that song again, it is a pathway to this moment. Savor the moment.

The more you practice, the more perfect moments you will notice.

Our life is made up of weeks, days, hours. How we remember that time is a choice. And like the treasured memory you've just recalled, you can create a whole library of wonderful times.

*Be aware of a perfect moment*
*Create your own memories for the future*
*Memories remind you there are better times ahead*

# 8

## THE WORTH OF WORRY

*Worry is an unresolved problem*

We all know the feeling. Butterflies that won't leave our stomach. A nagging thought something has been forgotten. Waking in the night and not going back to sleep from the chatter in our brain, hammering us with worse case scenarios at a time we are least able to do anything but feel more distressed.

Worry. Distracting, upsetting, and at times, debilitating.

But it has a purpose. A real and important role in our life. Learning how to use it to our advantage is the key.

Have you ever been driving and a warning light came on? Some random red light flashing at you. Are the brakes failing? Is the oil too low? What should you do? What most of us do is pull over when we can to see what is going on. The mechanically minded will recognize the problem from the light. The rest of us might get the car's manual out and compare the light to the list of diagnostics. We get the car repaired. We don't continue driving the car week in, week out, without addressing the warning. Not most people.

*Be aware of alerts to bigger problems*

Another example is an alarm sounding. A fire alarm in your house. At night. You wouldn't turn over and go back to sleep without investigating the cause, would you? More likely you'd hurry to see if it was a false alarm or a real emergency. If there's a fire, you take appropriate action. If not, you work out if the alarm is faulty and replace it.

But you take action. In both situations, you act.

The agitation we experience with worry is because we feel helpless. Unable to move. Caught by circumstances. This is where worry shows its worth. It is highlighting a problem.

*Problems require solutions*

Just as the fire alarm tells you there is a problem, so does worry.

How can we turn this around to work for us?

Getting to the source of the worry is the first step. Dig deep into the feeling and work on the wording until you can explain it in a sentence. Here's a common source of worry.

*I'm afraid I'll never have enough money to do what I want.*

An understandable concern that will play on the mind until it turns into worry.

Let's treat this as a beloved friend's problem instead of your own and help them solve it. What questions might you ask to get information to find a solution?

*How much money do you believe is 'enough' and what do you want this amount for?*

*Is there a way to reduce expenses to free up money?*
*Can you sell anything to boost your funds?*

*What steps might you take to increase your income from work, such as taking a course to help with a promotion, or changing career?*

*Are you able to be more self-sufficient, perhaps planting vegetables and learning to sew?*

Because you are treating this as someone else's problem to solve, you can ask questions you might otherwise ignore. Then, when you've asked and answered as much as you can, take stock.

Did you put a figure on how much money you want? If not, try asking how much you *need*, and see if the answer is there. Have you come up with some solutions?

More important. How do you feel?

Actively addressing a problem encourages our mind to see it differently. Rather than an endless cycle of 'what if' and 'I'll never', we begin to reframe the subject. Action makes worrying about something unnecessary.

Even if worry is about things outside our control it helps us to ask the questions. One little example is the worry there'll never be world peace. A question might be how we can change this. What would you answer? Can one person bring world peace? Most likely not. But each of us can practice kindness and teach acceptance. Big things happen because little things add up.

Practice turning worry into action. Use those uncomfortable feelings to get to the bottom of the problem. At the very least you can accept what you can change or control, and let the rest go. If you cannot control something, what point is there in worrying?

Should worry become so debilitating that these practical solutions don't help, or you struggle to function, please talk to your preferred medical practitioner to rule out underlying issues. This in itself is action.

> *Worry is an unresolved problem*
> *Treat the problem as if helping a dear friend*
> *Recognise what you can change and let the rest go*

# 9

## DREAMS TO DO

*A better time is ahead. What will you do first?*

The effect of recent events have rippled across the globe and impacted almost every aspect of our lives at this time. The things we've taken for granted are now restricted or unattainable. We feel uncertain about the future of travel, events, and much more.

But it won't be forever.

*This will pass*

There is benefit in looking ahead. Dreaming ahead.

Instead of using the word 'planning', *dreaming* seems more appropriate. Planning implies bookings and dates and money whereas dreaming about future costs nothing but time and imagination.

Many people called it a bucket list which is simply dreams to do.

In your heart of hearts, under ideal circumstances, what

do you long to experience in the future? For some it might be as simple as visiting a loved one. For others, viewing the northern lights from a boat in Norway.

*Why not have both?*

Finances and personal limitations aside, investigate the possibilities. The internet offers many resources so use them to design your dreams. Explore beautiful places near and far. Rainforests and valleys, misty beaches, and islands beneath a tropical sun. Grey days in London or a canal in Venice. The green of Ireland or gold of a desert.

You may not wish to travel. What intrigues you? Think of an experience you've secretly longed to try. White water rafting or parachuting? Attending a concert as a VIP guest? The only limit is your imagination at this point.

This is about expanding your belief in what is possible. Most people don't daydream enough. Yet it is healthy for our minds and good for our soul. As children, daydreaming helps our brains formulate ideas and fills ours hearts with adventure. We can do the same as adults.

Make your list. Have fun doing it. Always wanted to ride on a carousel but never did? Put it down. Camp alone on the beach? Add it. No matter where your mind takes you, add to your list and then enjoy searching for ways to make it happen in the future. Because we don't know what the future holds.

*Visit friends or family members in multiple places*
*Spend an afternoon swimming beneath a waterfall*
*Gaze at the stars from a hammock on a beach*
*Sail around Cape Horn*
*Travel on the Orient Express*
*Learn to scuba dive on the Great Barrier Reef*
*Swim with whales*
*Wander through ten museums*

*Sleep in an ice cave*
*Learn to cook with a celebrity chef*
*Write the book you keep hidden inside your heart*
*Dance under moonlight on a beach*

What will your list include? Ask your family and friends for ideas when you run out. Print it out, pin it up, add pictures. Surprise yourself.

*Remember how to daydream*
*Go will with ideas*
*Your future. Your dreams-to-do.*

## 10

# IT IS AROUND YOU, NOT INSIDE YOU

*This time will pass. Look within for sanctuary.*

Much of the happenings of these times are out of our hands. Not of our doing. Outside our control. Unless we are a senior decision maker, our role is to follow the recommendations and laws to protect ourselves and those around us.

Different regions have different rules. Even within countries, guidelines vary between states and areas and what might be okay in one place, is liable to fines in another.

Whether you are an essential worker or a person affected by strict shelter-in-place, your life has changed. And change, even longed for, positive change, is stressful, let alone change forced upon an unsuspecting society. How we shop and exercise, socialize and work is under a cloud of uncertainty and even confusion.

Should we allow the outside influences, the things we cannot control, dictate how we feel? Should we fall into despair because we expose ourselves to daily doses of bad news fed to us by the media? Social media is rife with keyboard experts and the information overload is overwhelming. How to tell fact from fallacy becomes exhausting.

Around us we see panic and worry and fear of the future.

Yet the future is what we can hold onto with hope and anticipation.

*This time will pass*

Our lives will become our own again. And now is the time to set ourselves up for a future with more to look forward to.

More happiness, because you've learned you are capable of change and have discovered your own power.

More appreciation of other people with their strengths and needs and humanness.

More excitement about what we once took for granted. We'll be travelling again, eating out, celebrating with our families and friends, planning. Yes, we'll be planning again.

You can count on yourself. You cannot control what happens outside but you most certainly can control what goes on inside. Feed your inner self with kindness and hope. Replace the diet of bad news with positive thoughts.

Create a peaceful place to retreat to when the outside gets too much. A private sanctuary of calm and resilience. An oasis.

Consider activities such as yoga. Get your hands dirty in rich soil in the garden. Meditate or pray. Walk when you can. Put your favorite music on and dance.

*You are not responsible for world events*
*Delight in the wonderful future ahead*
*Create a peaceful sanctuary inside yourself*

## 11

## DOING WELL WHEN THINGS GET TIGHT

*Finding true wealth*

When our lives tick over the way they normally do, we generally know what our income is from week to week, month to month, along with our expenses. Some of us live from pay check to pay check while others have a buffer in the bank, and others again are on a fixed income or almost none at all.

Regardless, when our environment changes, we are all affected one way or another. Work may disappear overnight. Others have more work but less time. Childcare arrangements and schooling are disrupted. All of these contribute to our budget needing an overhaul. Between countries, and even within a country, laws and decrees differ vastly on where we can go, what we can do, and how we can earn an income with so many restrictions.

For many, keeping money aside for unforeseen events is a priority. If our regular income is affected, this adds pressures we may not be able to manage without adapting to different ways of saving. How much should we sacrifice from our usual routine? Whether we have children, are newlyweds, retirees, or any number of other positions in life, taking stock of what we need is a great start.

*Is it a need or a want?*

They are not the same. We might want a new phone but do we need it? If your existing phone works, then possibly not.

Make a list of your income and outgoings. Use a notepad or a spreadsheet or download a free budgeting tool. There are heaps on the internet. Look for expenses you might not take much notice of, small amounts for subscriptions for example, including streaming services. Highlight what are actual necessities. Food, housing costs, repayments. Whatever you know are constants that must be paid to survive without creating future financial issues for yourself.

This done, take a critical look at expenses which don't affect the basic needs of shelter, food, clothing, transport for work/school, communication. You might be surprised with how many outgoings you can curtail and redirect your money into savings or where they are needed at the time.

*Change your relationship with money*

Whether you need to make one change or multiple, why not use this as an opportunity for more financial freedom? With many of us unable to leave our homes except for essential travel, and so much closed down, it seems a perfect time to consider how to make permanent changes for our long-term benefit. You can streamline your life.

Do you have a garden or balcony? Even in a small space, you can grow herbs, vegetables, and fruit. Dig around on the internet for ideas before digging the ground. Most regions have a local social media page for gardening and welcome newbies with questions. Some people offer seeds and cuttings to swap or buy cheaply and will advise on what grows best in the local climate. Small spaces are ideal for vertical gardens which can be homemade if you want to try a small building project. Homegrown food tastes fabulous, is free of chemicals if you do a little work against pests, and is great for children to learn about. With the internet at our fingertips, recipes, and ideas for freezing, bottling, and swapping are sure to inspire you.

*Discover the delight of homegrown and made*

Speaking of food, eating out is both expensive and not always possible. Why not have a night in? Create a menu, set the table with your best cutlery and crockery, and even get dressed up as if heading somewhere special. Need menu ideas? Visit the websites of restaurants you've either been to, or would love to eat at. Even if you don't have the recipe or a chef at home to make the meal look the same, you'll be motivated to create your own version. If you have a few people in the family at home, give everyone a job so one person doesn't become cook, waiter, and dishwasher.

Another lovely idea is a gourmet picnic outside, even in your garden. Find a nice spot in the shade, lay out a blanket and share a meal made from the heart. Relax with birdsong as your music.

If the food budget is tight, supermarkets usually have discounted stock so it is worth asking a team member when they normally reduce close-to-date products. Anything you can't use straight away can go into the freezer, or be pre-cooked in larger than normal amounts and frozen. Saves on time as well to have a few ready-made meals to heat. Small specialist shops often are better stocked with fresh products and well-priced as are farmer's markets when trading.

Love reading? A lot of libraries and bookshops are closed right now and online shopping can prove expensive. One good option is a reading subscription. Although subscriptions are not always good value, those where you pay a small amount monthly to have access to unlimited reads is a small cost if you read a lot. Some online retailers offer reading apps free and sometimes introductory free trials. You can also search for free books on the same retailers and places like BookBub, which is a free-to-join reader website. If you prefer paperbacks, look for local groups of booklovers, café's and community groups who do swaps.

*Get creative with entertainment*

Search for special events on television, YouTube or similar. Some performances of bands, orchestras, ballets, and musicals are being made available to enjoy. Turn the lights off as if having a night at the theatre. Or discover an old series or movies from another era.

Cutting costs doesn't have to be an exercise in misery. Keep what is important but regularly re-evaluate the situation. Giving up or reducing fast food, subscriptions to most live streaming channels, or habits such as smoking might not have been on your to-do list. But if it makes financial sense to look at their real worth to you, surely they need scrutiny about the part they play with your health, time, and wellbeing.

Changing doesn't need to be immediate. Getting used to more homemade meals rather than store-bought might take a while, but the long-term gains are huge. Less artificial additives and harmful preservatives in your body, fresher ingredients, cost, the satisfaction of making your own meals.

Savings you learn to make now will make a difference to your future.

Give every change some time and your best effort and you

might very well decide to keep those changes for the rest of your life.

*Get a true picture of what you need*
*Seek out different ways to enjoy your interests*
*Be bold about change. Give it a good go.*

12
——————————

## SILVER LININGS

*Positive thoughts help our body feel happiness*

Imagine a storm. Laden with rain, clouds scuttling across the sky. Lightning flashes within those clouds before breaking free to fork to the ground, ferocious and destructive. Thunder booms across the atmosphere and when the rain begins, it is a deluge. Our plans for the day may be ruined by the storm. There might be damage from wind, hail, or lightning. We huddle under shelter until the storm passes.

When it does, we emerge again. The air is fresh. Dams and reservoirs replenished. Trees watered. Puddles abound. Sun breaks through the clouds and we get on with our day.

Storms change things. If a tree falls on a house, it is for the worse. If it refills the water troughs on your drought-stricken land, it is for the better. Either way, a storm doesn't care about your plans or whether you are caught in the middle of it without shelter. It just is. And the sun shining through clouds is our reminder there is always hope.

*How do we find the upside of negatives?*

Each situation brings its own challenges. The global pandemic has touched every person in some way. What possible silver lining could a wide-spread virus have? Lives lost. Jobs gone. International travel all but stopped. Borders closed, some within countries. Our way of life changed with no say from us.

Consider this. With the massive reduction in transport and industry, pollution levels have fallen. For the health of the planet—humans, animals, land, water, air—this has far reaching implication and benefits. How wonderful if this helps us move faster toward alternative fuels and sustainable living for everyone.

Many people are turning to growing their own produce. Rather than our food travelling from the other side of the country, or even the world, imagine the freshness of locally grown. Making your own soup from pumpkins grown in your garden beats tinned soup any day.

Teaching our children how to grow food and cook it is a real silver lining in this age of fast food and disposable packaging. This rare opportunity to educate in practical ways is every bit as important as school lessons. It is future proofing.

*This is a rare chance to see what is possible*

Where else can we find silver linings? A change in marital status, for example, is distressing and disruptive regardless of the reason or who initiated it. One important part of our life is over. Perhaps the biggest part of our life. It is more than two people going separate ways. Children, friends, property, pets, businesses. All will be affected. So where is the positive in this?

If the marriage wasn't happy, even on one side, then your

silver lining is ahead in future happiness. Even if you wanted the marriage to continue, you still have a wonderful future. Look for the things you love and didn't give enough time to. A hobby, career, friends. Or just time for you. Reading late, or sleeping in. Or being first for once. Write down the things you want from life and see how this new situation might align with them.

Our minds respond to positive thoughts by helping our bodies feel better so seeking those silver linings is important. If we learn to look beyond the initial disappointment, sadness, or grief then we are working toward healing. Patience and perseverance are the keys.

*Is there always a silver lining? What about losing a loved one?*

What greater sadness could there be? When our heart is broken, grief plays a necessary role of transition. Through its stages, we experience intense emotions, strong enough to affect us physically at times. Others may offer words of comfort, words about the positives of the lost one. Only you will know when to begin comforting yourself.

It may not feel real when someone says your lost one 'will always be with you'. But one day you'll notice the sunrise or a shooting star, feel the brush of a breeze against your cheek, or hear a song special to them. Then you might see the glimmer of a silver lining. It wasn't that you lost them, it was that you loved them. Memories are real and the way we stay connected, even after loss are real too.

Remember the storm. It just is. No thought of what it does or who it impacts. We know each storm will pass. We grow stronger by weathering storms because our belief in ourselves to survive whatever life throws at us intensifies. Silver linings are always there.

*Be strong in the storm for it will pass*
*Actively seek the positives in your life*
*Practice patience and let yourself have time*

## 13

# ACCEPT REGRETS

*Why cling to something that has no purpose?*

You've made a mistake. Said something you wish you hadn't. Jumped in when waiting was called for. Missed an opportunity which won't come again. Didn't speak up and know you should have said something.

We all mess up. We also all misjudge situations, lose faith in ourselves, overthink, and forget things.

How do you respond to making an error which affects some important part of your life? Typical responses range from anger at ourselves to disappointment. Frustration to sadness. It depends upon what has happened and who we are. Most of the time, those feelings diminish over a short period of time. We fix what we can and move on.

Sometimes we replay an event over and over in our minds, not only as it happened but in various scenarios we could have experienced had we done things differently. We fixate on the lead up, the moment itself, and the fallout.

Rather than moving on, the memory becomes a vinyl record of regret. It turns and turns and there is no way to end the cycle. This interferes with our sleep, with our interaction with others, and also with our relationship with ourselves.

*Regret can harm us*

When this happens, our view of the situation becomes slanted as negativity pinpoints every minute detail rather than letting us evaluate it with some distance.

An example is this scenario: you have an important meeting to attend at work, but you forget and miss it. At this meeting, a promotion is announced for the job you want. It goes to someone else.

Your initial dismay when you remember the meeting turns to guilt because you were asked to attend. Your supervisor may have been in trouble with their boss for your lack of attendance. More than this, the longed-for promotion is someone else's. Your employer must have changed their mind about giving it to you when you failed to attend.

Before you know it, you are consumed with regret because the promotion meant more money and responsibility. This feels like the worst mistake of your life. Not only for the effects on others, but because it stopped you attaining your goal of the life-changing promotion.

**Stop. Rewind.**

Let's look at it differently. Why did you forget the meeting? Your child was unwell overnight and when you finally got to sleep, it was to wake with a foggy brain still focused on their wellbeing. By being with them, your child was comforted and knew they were safe because their parent was there. They will remember this in a positive way. This is good. The response from your employer showed you the company doesn't have a good work/life balance policy and taking on more responsibility would mean longer hours for not a lot more pay.

This is one of thousands of situations where we might feel regret. But almost everything can be turned around when we zoom out a bit.

Imagine your best friend had this regret. You'd talk them through it, point out what might have been out of their control and what benefits have arisen from the event. You'd tell them to be kind to themselves. To forgive and let go. If this is what you'd say to your friend, then say it to yourself.

*The key is self-forgiveness*

Even if what we regret was completely our doing and had far reaching repercussions with no visible upside, you still need to forgive yourself.

Eating yourself up is not healthy. It hurts us mentally, emotionally, and physically. It may stop us taking chances or saying what needs saying from fear of reliving this regret. When we've hurt another person, we can apologize. Offer to do something to make it right or at least show we've learnt a powerful lesson. Whatever the outcome, a time comes when self-forgiveness is more important than gripping this pain.

Regret is useful only in teaching us to be more aware. It serves no purpose becoming a circle of distress. Regretting something will not undo it. It will not fix it.

The time you waste in this cycle of anger, sadness, disappointment or grief is time you can't recover. Stop now. Breath deep and let the regret go as you exhale. Tell yourself you are done regretting and are back to living fully and boldly. Accept you made an error. Accept that holding it over your own head and heart is doing nothing to improve the situation. Accept regret for what it is. A reminder you are human with flaws. But one also with heart and happiness and so much to discover ahead.

*Offer an apology. Repair what is possible.
Treat yourself as a beloved friend. Forgive yourself.
Move forward. It is all we have.*

14

---

## A SECRET OASIS

*Invite yourself to a place of calm and clarity*

Where do you go when you want to be mentally alone? To think without interruption, to daydream or plan. To meditate or pray. Do you have a special place and routine or try to grab a moment here or there when the house is quiet?

Consider what an oasis is. A small place where water springs from the ground, turning desert into a garden. There may be trees or other plants. It creates its own micro ecosystem as birds and animals are drawn to its relief from heat and barren land.

These havens are found around the world in desolate and unexpected spots. Weary travelers rest and refill their energy and resources from the spring or stream. These oases save lives.

In our modern world, most people have access to fresh water and shelter, particularly in first world countries. We may already have a lush garden to enjoy. So why do we need an oasis?

Our lives are busy. Hectic at times. Filled with other people's needs and our own duties. We heap work upon ourselves as well as social and family commitments. Whether we run our day on a timetable or on the run, time for ourselves is often down the list of things to do. Even hobbies and interests require a certain active energy and attention.

*We need to refill our well*

No matter how happy and full our life is, quiet time is vital for wellbeing. And if we're in an unhappy state, a mental oasis is like a buoy in a storm.

In a quiet, calm place, our thoughts can drift. We become aware of our breathing, long deep breaths all the way to our stomach and slowly back out. If we have muscle pain or other discomfort, we can focus on that instead of pushing it away because we're too busy. Recognizing we hurt is step one to taking action to address the reason.

We can talk to ourselves. Ask how we are doing and what we need. If you ask and listen closely for an answer, your mind and body may surprise you.

Pay attention to something simple, like the sound of water or gentle music or your own breathing. As your mind slows down, you'll find it easier to look at stressful problems with less urgency. Concentrating on something small and neutral helps us manage bigger worries.

*Focus on something beautiful*

Sounds inviting, doesn't it? Even a few minutes in our secret oasis refills our metaphorical well. The shade cools us, and the gentle splash of water soothes. However you visualize your oasis, carve out a little time to visit it regularly.

Where is this special place? It lives in our mind but the setting matters. Depending upon our situation, we might need to leave the house or find creative ways to make a spot for ourselves. Should our circumstances not provide a suitable physical oasis or prevent travelling to one, don't give up. Think outside the box. Here's a few suggestions.

*The garden beneath a tree*
*On a balcony*
*Sitting or walking on a quiet beach*
*In a parked car*
*Alone in our bedroom*
*On a park bench*
*Using headphones connected to gentle sounds or no sounds*
*During a bath or shower*
*Gazing at the night sky or a sunrise*

Rituals help our mind prepare to visit. These might be as simple as shutting a door, closing your eyes, and telling yourself it is oasis time. Or as elaborate as preparing a bubble bath with candles. The more you practice, the easier sinking into and enjoying the feeling of clarity, calmness and self-awareness will become.

Over time, you'll find yourself drawing on those feelings when dealing with problems or stress. If we learn to go to our oasis, our 'happy place' at will, then difficult challenges, loss, or distress may be a bit easier to manage. We all need our secret place to visit.

*Use your secret oasis to refill your emotional well*
*Experiment with the setting*
*Ask yourself what you need and listen to the answer*

## 15

## BE FEARLESS

*It is never too late to learn to fly*

In today's rapidly changing arena, fear is hard to avoid. Fear of what is happening around us. Fear of how this affects us now and in the future. Fear of losing our jobs, income, homes, family. So much fear.

We are also accustomed to fear from a lifetime of seeing and hearing, sometimes experiencing, frightening situations. Home invasions, wars, terrorism, bullying, typhoons and tornadoes. We may have grown up in or be in a family where violence is accepted

There are other fears as well. Fear of failure. Fear of missing out. Phobia-driven fears of spiders, storms, the dark, or heights. Television, entertainment, social media, and word of mouth contribute to filling our minds and hearts with fear that one day something terrible will happen to us.

Fear does serve a purpose. When we are in danger, being afraid forces us to take action to protect ourselves, whether it be running away, hiding, or fighting back. In such situations our brain is wired to look after us, heighten our senses, keep us alert until the danger passes. It is basic and effective.

*Low-level fear has no place in our life*

There is a difference between life-saving fear, and low-level fear. The second kind is all the worries in the back of our mind, the fears not involved with protecting us. Being afraid you'll miss out on seeing a new release film first or fall off a cliff when you live on a plain are irrational and not helpful. They take time and energy from positive parts of your life.

We've talked about worrying. It serves the purpose of alerting us to something we need to attend to. Worry is an unresolved problem. Once you act, the worry evaporates.

Fear is the same. It only belongs where action is required. Flight, fight, or freeze. If a fear cannot be categorized into one of those states, then look critically at why it is there. Write a list of your fears and whether a response to them happening would be fight, flight, or freeze. If not, try to understand how and why they affect you. You might find a few you can let go.

*Learn to see the difference*

Living fearlessly is to live your life to the full. Take chances on your dreams. Dare to make mistakes. Understand you will have rejections and some will hurt. Plan to go whitewater rafting one day, or skydiving. Ask for a raise. Stand up for yourself and your loved ones in a calm and firm manner. Be prepared to leave a situation, whether work, family, or relationship, if it is toxic. Try new foods. Write that book.

How sad to live a life without all the things we've talked about. Without joy. Missing out on creating new future memories. Never starting the dream-to-do list let alone fulfilling it.

Now is the perfect time to be fearless. Take hold of your

life by delving into your dreams, hopes, needs. Look forward. Find happiness in your own company. Accept nothing less than love and respect from those close to you. Ask for help and offer it freely. Join a theatre group, learn a new language, swim in the ocean, learn to fly. Above all, love yourself.

*Embrace a fearless approach to problems*
*Take chances on living life to the full*
*Have no regrets and love yourself*

## 16

# GRATITUDE, JOY AND RESILIENCE

*Three pillars of strength*

How wonderful to be the recipient of appreciation. For someone to thank us for being there for them or doing something to help out.

The look of surprise on a toddler's face when they splash in a puddle for the first time turns to delight as they jump, run, and make a wonderful mess.

Despite no support, we gain the degree we worked years to attain.

Gratitude, joy, and resilience. Three essential qualities for a happy life. All three come naturally to some people, but for many, one or more may require attention and skill-building to fully benefit from them. The benefit of developing these as part of our day to day lives outweighs any effort it takes.

When someone gives us a gift, a promotion, a compliment, we usually respond with 'thank you'. It makes us feel good, even special, to receive something nice, whether expected or not. This is one kind of gratitude. Another is our appreciation of the good in our lives, from the beauty of a sunset to the smile on a loved one's face.

Sometimes, our past may hinder our natural gratitude. A hard life with many struggles might leave us wondering what there is to be thankful of. On the other hand, some people have a strong sense of entitlement. If you believe the world owes you a living, fancy clothes, or the latest phone, then being grateful may not be a natural response.

*Appreciate the gifts life brings*

Feeling grateful sends powerful messages to our brain. Think of one thing you are grateful of. A simple thing such as having food in the fridge or being loved. Focus on your emotions when you are grateful. Say it aloud with meaning. "I am grateful for the people who love me." Did you feel your heart lift a little? Find yourself smiling? Gratitude is healthy for us and helps us see our own world in a unique light.

If it is a struggle to find anything at first, dig deep. Search for little things and build upon them. Practice observing your life and discovering what is a gift. Life. Air we can breathe. Enough food. Expand to your loved ones. Or past loved ones. Gratitude works for past happiness and gifts as well as current ones. Accept these gifts.

*Gratitude will fill our hearts*

Joy is more than happiness, although happiness is part of joy. A joyful spirit is key to long term contentment and inner strength. It sustains us through difficult times and sadness.

As with gratitude, we need to seek out what brings joy.

As important is what does not bring joy. Even the most joyful of people may become depleted and overwhelmed by excessive outside negativities. We have a lot of control over what we permit to invade our thoughts, but it does take effort. Become aware of how much time you dedicate to current affairs, news reports, and social media.

So often, there is an overload of information, much of it slanted for sensationalism. This plays on our minds. Even when we discard information as flawed or unworthy, it still takes up space. Cutting down on exposure to negative input is like cutting down a rotten tree. Fresh air and sunlight replace it.

Once you know what doesn't bring joy, work as hard on what does, and increase your time in those areas. Most of all, learn about yourself and appreciate who you are as a person and the joy you bring others.

*Never underestimate the power of joyfulness*

Obstacles are a part of life. When we learn to walk, we fall over a lot until our balance improves. Before we know it, we're running. As a child, we don't see obstacles as barriers to what we want. Without boundaries from our parents, we'd go over and around and under anything in our way. Our resilience, at least for a while, is inborn.

As adults, most of us have lost that natural ability to get back up after a fall. Our upbringing, society, and individual temperaments dictate how we approach a problem. Giving up is easier than persevering for too many people.

Resilience is about bouncing back from a roadblock. Being able to reset after a rejection. Taking a different approach to see what works best. Persisting when nothing else but hard work gets a result. It is also about knowing when to stop and change direction. Some things are not worth your time and effort and recognizing those may save heartache and money.

*Make resilience into your secret superpower*

Practice resilience by changing how you think. Be aware

of negative thoughts and rechannel them into positives. Switch your focus. Learn from mistakes. Failing is not a bad thing. If toddlers stopped trying after their first fall, they'd still be crawling as adults. Keep an open mind to a problem. Look for ways around, over, or under the challenge. Ask for help but maintain control over your own projects. Recognize your skills and develop them as needed. Remember to laugh instead of frowning. Turn worry lines into laughter lines.

Gratitude, joy and resilience are positive, powerful aspects of life which hold us up in difficult times and gives us strength to face life by depending upon ourselves. Choose positive words to balance the negative. Repeat powerful affirmations when you meditate, visit your oasis, or feel stress. "I'm capable and strong." "I can do this." Believe in yourself.

*Draw gratitude into your daily life*
*Fill your days with positives and thrive on joy*
*Believe in yourself and follow your dreams*

# AFTERWORD

I set out to write this short book to help during times of deep stress, upsets or concerns. For me, it is like sitting across a table with a dear friend and talking about problems over a coffee.

If you've gained some comfort or hope from reading my words, then I am content. My belief is in paying-it-forward and this is my small way to express gratitude to the people in my life who made a difference.

Live your best life and go into the future fearless and joyful.
Believe in yourself.
I do.

**Phillipa Nefri Clark**
*(Writing as Ronen Groves)*

## ABOUT THE AUTHOR

Phillipa (who has written this under pen name Ronan Groves) lives just outside a beautiful town in country Victoria, Australia. She also lives in the many worlds of her imagination and stockpiles stories beside her laptop.
She writes from the heart about love, dreams, secrets, discovery, the sea, the world as she knows it… or wishes it could be. She loves happy endings, heart-pounding suspense, and characters who stay with you long after the final page.
With a passion for music, the ocean, animals, nature, reading, and writing, she is often found in the vegetable garden pondering a new story.

www.phillipaclark

Free short book when you join Phillipa's newsletter (books, pets, gardens, puzzles, first-looks and competitions).

## BY PHILLIPA NEFRI CLARK

**Rivers End Mystery Romances**

The Stationmaster's Cottage

Jasmine Sea

The Secrets of Palmerston House

The Christmas Key

Taming the Wind

Or read books 1-4 in one collection

The Rivers End Collection

**The Charlotte Dean Mysteries**

Deadly Start

Deadly Falls

Deadly Secrets

Deadly Past

The Giving Tree

**Daphne Jones Mysteries**

Daph on the Beach

Till Daph Do Us Part

The Shadow of Daph

Tales of Life and Daph

or read books 1-3 in one collection

The Daphne Jones Mysteries

A Perfect Danger

(Bindarra Creek Mystery Romance)

Tangled in Tinsel - coming soon

(Bindarra Creek Christmas Romance)

**Maple Gardens Matchmakers**

The Heart Match

The Christmas Match (coming soon)

Doctor Grok's Peculiar Shop Short Story Collection

(A bit of fantasy with a twist of magic)

Last Known Contact

(A gripping standalone crime/romantic suspense)

Simple Words for Troubled Times

(Short non-fiction happiness and comfort book)

**Prefer Audiobooks?**

The Stationmaster's Cottage

Jasmine Sea

The Secrets of Palmerston House

Last Known Contact

Simple Words for Troubled Times

Deadly Start

Deadly Falls

Deadly Secrets

Deadly Past

The Giving Tree

Till Daph Do Us Part